TESTIMONIALS

"A lot of time and effort has gone into this guide. May every moment be worth the value of a life being saved. God truly is in your life, Doris, and He filled you with the knowledge from on high to save another downtrodden soul. Much more to come."

Gwendolyn Angry
Retired School Teacher

"It is clear this book was written to benefit new and existing parents with pre- and school-age children. I believe the author intends to provide guidance, advice, education, and, most importantly, enhance children to be positively successful in their lives. While reading this book, I found it to be very informative to parents, relatives, friends, and the community to provide support to African-American males and females towards developing their fullest potential."

Rhonda Hardrick. Ed.D.

"Doris Barren's background experience and knowledge shows in the guide. Her ability to want to see real change in parents and their children is admirable. I agree with the necessity and validity of this book and guide at this point. My parents were definitely my role models, always picking my friends and dates. As an adult, I learned to appreciate my parents' strict Christian home where I was raised. Yes, my schoolteachers helped in the process, and also my church teachers, to help me grow to be a productive member of society."

Naomi Markham
Servant of God

CHANGE YOUR MINDSET /
SAVE YOUR CHILD

SAVING OUR CHILDREN BY HEALING OURSELVES

MY MINDSET-TRANSFORMATION GUIDE

DORIS BARREN

Halo
PUBLISHING
INTERNATIONAL

ISBN: 978-1-63765-179-7
Registration Number: TXu 2-291-119

Halo Publishing International, LLC
www.halopublishing.com

Printed and bound in the United States of America

ACKNOWLEDGMENTS

I could not have completed this guide without my faith and the help and support of my family members and friends. They took the time to read and share their thoughts and ideas. I will be forever grateful for their support.

Contents

PREFACE

I published *Change Your Mindset/Save Your Child: Saving Our Children By Healing Ourselves*, which this guide supports, earlier this year. It was a years-long project that finally came to fruition during the isolation we all endured in 2020 because of the pandemic caused by the COVID-19 virus. After it was published, I realized that, as a stand-alone, it didn't do enough to help those who wanted to find a way to improve their lives. I developed this guide to help fill that gap. As I did before, I used my experience as a wife, parent, grandparent, great-grandparent, and substitute teacher/tutor and my research to help me develop the questions, charts, and accompanying exercises that are part of each chapter.

The guide chapters are companions to the chapters in the book. I purposely aligned the chapters to expound on the topics discussed in the book. My goal is to work with you who commit to using this guide to help you transform your mindset and, subsequently, your lives. I am, figuratively, taking these steps with you in each chapter. I provide uplifting resources that I hope will inspire, help keep you focused, and give you the strength to complete this journey. I relied on my faith in God to guide me throughout this phase of my commitment to you. At the end of each chapter, I provide a section for reflection and any ideas or thoughts you may want to capture before going on to the next chapter.

Prepare to be honest with yourself as you respond to the chapter questions and statements you encounter. I also encourage you to choose a person you respect and who exhibits positive character traits identified in the book to take this journey (literally) with you as your *Accountability Partner.* Your Accountability Partner will play a crucial role in your mindset-transformation journey. Before you choose, read *chapters four and eight* in the book. When you have identified the person you want to help you, be sure to discuss your goals and ask them to support you. They will need to read the book and review this guide to understand how significant their role is to your success.

The guide's design supports individuals who plan to take this journey independently (with your Accountability Partner) or in a workshop setting. In either scenario, commitment and dedication to achieving your goals are critical to your success.

Remember, this is a marathon, not a race. The changes you desire will come, but not overnight. Before you begin the work of transforming your mindset, take the time to read and sign **My Mindset-Transformation Commitment Declaration** in the introduction. By committing to the work ahead of you in writing, you show how serious you are about achieving your desired results.

- If you are hesitant or have doubts about this undertaking, please consider the following:
- Former President Barack Obama said the following, "Change will not come if we wait for some other person or some other time. We are the ones we've been waiting for. We are the change that we seek." (***https://www.brainyquote.com/quotes/barack_obama_409128***) In this case, *you are the change you seek!*

- Your children learn what they are forced to live every day. What do you want them to learn?
- Your future does not have to be driven by your past, but you must make a choice.
- No one can disrespect you without your permission.

You are not alone.

INTRODUCTION

This document is the companion to my book, *Change Your Mindset/Save Your Child: Saving Our Children by Healing Ourselves.* I created it to provide you with a resource that you can use to:

1. Determine what changes you *want/need* to make based on how your mindset affects your child(ren)'s growth and well-being.

2. Guide you through the process of understanding and documenting what changes you should make and how you can plan to accomplish them.

3. Serve as a *living/evolving support tool* that you can change and update as you progress towards achieving your desired outcomes.

NOTE: To gain the full benefit from the chapter exercises in this guide, I encourage you to read the book *first.*

As you go forward, please remember this:

1. Change is not easy, especially changing *ourselves.* It takes time and *patience.* We didn't get the way we are now overnight. We won't change overnight. But every positive outcome begins with that *first* step. If you are reading this planning guide or the book itself, *you have already taken that first step!!* I applaud you for your honesty and willingness to move out of your comfort zone and embrace the future with a *changed* mindset.

2. Here is where "Begin with the End in Mind" (Stephen Covey, The Seven Habits of Highly Effective People) is truly important. What do you want your family's result to be? As you complete the upcoming charts and chapter exercises and answer the accompanying questions, think about how you and your children want your family's transformation to look. How will it be different than it is now?

3. None of us is perfect. We ALL fall short, but we cannot and should not allow our past missteps to keep us from reaching for the blessings that God is WAITING to bestow upon our families and us. We owe it to ourselves and even more to our children, who are our future.

4. **YOU** are your children's first and most important role model. *They learn what they live every day.* *What do you want them to learn? Remember:*

    a. Positivity begets positivity. Negativity begets negativity.
        Love begets love. Hate begets hate.

THE DECISION IS YOURS!!!

LET THE TRANSFORMATION BEGIN!!

I pray that with God's grace and guidance you find this document not only beneficial but *essential* to your ongoing growth as a *Positive Role Model* for all of the children you influence and help to develop a positive mindset and outlook.

REMEMBER:

A NEGATIVE MIND CANNOT
LEAD TO A POSITIVE LIFE!!

My *Mindset-Transformation* Commitment Declaration

I, _____, commit to following the guidelines outlined in this Mindset-Transformation Guide to achieve the outcomes I desire for myself and my family. I commit to being honest with my answers when I complete the charts and other exercises provided in each chapter. I commit to working with _____, my Accountability Partner, to ensure I stay on track and achieve the desired outcomes for myself and my family. I know this journey I'm about to begin, which will transform my mindset and outlook, is not easy and the results will not be immediate. However, achieving my desired future is worth the time and hard work it requires. I know that my changed life begins with my changed mindset.

I make this commitment without reservation or hesitation on this date: _____.

_____   _____

Print Your Name   Sign Your Name

CHAPTER ONE

We Are What We Think

"You will never change your life until you change something you do daily."
—**Mike Murdock,** *The Leadership Secrets of Jesus*

Directions: If you are happy with the way things are going in your life right now, skip this chapter and go on to chapter two. If you are *NOT* satisfied with your life right now, complete the following chart:

1. Using the categories below, write down what you are *unhappy* about (issues).

2. Review the components of a Positive Mindset vs. a Negative Mindset (pp. 13-17 in the book).

3. What actions/nonactions are you contributing to the issue(s)? *Please be honest with yourself!!*

4. What current *mindset* are your actions/nonactions demonstrating? Do they need to change?

5. Identify someone you admire and trust who demonstrates a positive approach and ask for their help working through the issues you identify in the chart below. They can offer perspectives you may not recognize (this person can serve as your Accountability Partner).

Use the chart on the next page to document your responses.

CHANGING *MY* MINDSET SELF-ASSESSMENT

Category	Issue(s)	My contributing actions / nonactions	Current mindset (*P* or *N*)
Faith			
Family			
Friends			
Others			
Career			

After completing your self-assessment, take a few minutes to review your responses. Compare your actions/nonactions in each category to the *current* mindset they reveal in the last column.

Answer the following questions:

1. What does this tell you about your current mindset?

2. What experiences in your life have impacted how you currently react to the issues you identified in your Self-Assessment?

3. How have these experiences affected how you currently interact with your family, friends, and others you encounter?

CHAPTER ONE REFLECTION AND NOTES

ENTER YOUR THOUGHTS/IDEAS/CONCERNS/REVELATIONS HERE:

_____

_____

_____

_____

_____

_____

_____

_____

_____

CHAPTER TWO

Walk a Mile in My Shoes

Photo by Anete Lusina from Pexels

1. How well do you know and understand what your children think of your current family environment?

2. What kind of behaviors do you see? What is your current reaction to your children when they misbehave?

3. When was the last time you asked your children how they feel about issues your family may be experiencing? Did you listen to them without interrupting? Did you ask why they think that way?

4. Have you provided your children with a family culture that helps them feel it's okay to voice their true feelings without being punished? Remember, children respond to the family culture *you* establish.

5. What actions/nonactions from your self-assessment in chapter one could be contributing to any behavior issues with your children?

6. How do you plan to address these actions/nonactions *with* your children?

Use the chart on the next page to answer these questions.

MY *FAMILY-CULTURE* ASSESSMENT

Question	Response	What needs to change?
1. How well do you know and understand what your children think of your current family environment?		
2. What kind of behaviors do you see? What is your current reaction to your children when they misbehave?		
3. When was the last time you asked your children how they feel about issues your family may be experiencing? Did you listen to them without interrupting? Did you ask why they think that way?		
4. Have you provided your children with a family culture that helps them feel it's okay to voice their true feelings without being punished? Remember, children respond to the family culture you establish.		
5. What actions/nonactions from your self-assessment in chapter one could be contributing to any behavior issues with your children?		

The following resources may also be helpful as you and your children work *together* to improve your family culture:

1. If your child is showing signs of getting into the gang culture (the friends they choose can offer a clue here—*review chapter six*), this resource may be able to help: *https://bit.ly/3wOzbDTGangs-and-Teens.*

2. Don't forget, our churches offer support and counseling in all aspects of parenting.

3. When you begin to feel the sheer weight of your parenting responsibilities and aren't sure how much more you can handle on your own, check out this resource: *https://bit.ly/3wSJaInParenting-Support.*

4. If you have children with special needs and you're not sure where to turn for help, start here: *https://bit.ly/3266OWHYouth-With-Special-Needs.*

CHAPTER TWO REFLECTION AND NOTES

ENTER YOUR THOUGHTS/IDEAS/CONCERNS/REVELATIONS HERE:

_____

_____

_____

_____

_____

_____

_____

_____

_____

CHAPTER THREE

The School-to-Prison Pipeline

"It is easier to build strong children than to repair broken men."
—Frederick Douglass

How much do you know about the criminal/juvenile justice system and how it can affect your children? In this case, what we don't know *can hurt* our children and us— *but especially our children*. Consider the following news reports that describe a *6-year-old girl*, **who is** crying and screaming for help as an Orlando police officer *arrests* her at school, and her grandmother's response. The incident occurred on September 19, 2019.

1. This is the 6-year-old girl's *grandmother's* response to the incident shortly after it occurred: *https://bit.ly/329kWP3Grandmother-Responds* (Tess Sheets, Orlando Sentinel News, October 2, 2019).

2. **The report on the actual incident and the outcome is:** https://bit.ly/3Hn7abrSix-Year-Old-Arrested (Grace Toohey, *Orlando Sentinel News*, February 24, 2021).

This child was barely out kindergarten when the incident occurred, and she most likely will be made a part of the criminal/juvenile justice system before she has had a chance to begin her learning journey. How did this happen? Could it have been prevented?

What is *our* role in helping our children avoid these insidious traps? Forewarned is forearmed.

Consider the following questions:

1. If you have family or friends incarcerated, how old were they when they first became part of the criminal justice system? What were their crimes? Have you discussed it with your children?

2. Have your children gotten into trouble in school? If so, what led to it? What was the outcome?

3. How well are your children performing in school? Do you monitor them?

4. Do you have a good relationship with their teachers?

5. How often do you discuss your children's performance with their teachers?

6. Have you spent any time with your children to determine where they might be having problems? What have you done to get help for them?

7. Do you know what your children's school's discipline policies are? Have you discussed them with your children to help them understand how their behavior in class can affect their future success in school and in their lives?

Review your Family-Culture Assessment chart in chapter two. Does your current family culture provide a positive nurturing environment for your children?

8. Does your children's school advocate Zero-Tolerance or Restorative practices? Do you know the difference?

9. How do you plan to help steer your children away from the criminal/juvenile justice system traps?

Use your answers to the questions above to help you create the following **Action Plan.** As you complete the plan, remember this: Many of our children are only *ONE BAD DECISION* away from making themselves *voluntary* members of the *INCARCERATED* population in our criminal/juvenile justice system.

What will you do to help keep that from happening to your children?

MY FAMILY'S ACTION PLAN FOR
SCHOOL-TO-PRISON AVOIDANCE

QUESTION	MY RESPONSE	HOW I PLAN TO ADDRESS IT WITH MY CHILDREN
1. If you have family or friends incarcerated, how old were they when they first became part of the criminal justice system? What were their crimes?		
2. Have your children gotten into trouble in school? If so, what led to it? What was the outcome?		
3. How well are your children performing in school? Do you monitor them? Do you have a good relationship with their teachers?		
4. How often do you discuss your children's performance with their teachers?		
5. Have you spent any time with your children to determine where they might be having problems? What have you done to get help for them?		

QUESTION	MY RESPONSE	HOW I PLAN TO ADDRESS IT WITH MY CHILDREN
6. Do you know what your children's school's discipline policies are? Have you discussed them with your children to help them understand how their behavior in class can affect their future success in school? *(Review your Family-Culture Assessment chart. Does your family culture support them?)*		
7. Does your children's school advocate Zero-Tolerance or Restorative practices? Do you know the difference?		

The following resources will give more information on question 7:

a. *https://bit.ly/2YNlXL6Restorative-Practices*

b. *The Little Book of Race and Restorative Justice ("Race, Restorative Justice, and Schools," pp. 42-57), Fania E. Davis*

CHAPTER THREE REFLECTION AND NOTES

ENTER YOUR THOUGHTS/IDEAS/CONCERNS/REVELATIONS HERE:

_____

_____

_____

_____

_____

_____

_____

_____

_____

CHAPTER FOUR

Choose Your Heroes Wisely

*"If we don't invest now in building **character** in children,*
*we will surely invest more tomorrow in trying to **repair** adults."*
—Michael Josephson

We should be our children's *first and most important* heroes!!

1. Review your responses to chapter one's *Changing MY Mindset Self-Assessment.* What does it show about you? Have you been a positive role model for your children up until now? (Remember, none of us is perfect. We all fall short at times).

2. What, if any, changes do you need to make to be the kind of role model your children deserve to see and emulate? (Remember, our children *learn what they live every day.* If you completed the self-assessment in chapter one, you will have a head start in answering this question).

3. Do you know who your children's friends are? Do they demonstrate the kind of behaviors that represent a positive mindset?

4. Have you educated your children on distinguishing between a positive role model and a "wolf in sheep's clothing"? Can *you* recognize the difference?

5. Are there any adult relatives, friends, or community members who, you believe, would be good examples of positive role models for your children? How often do they interact with your family? Remember this verse from the NIV version of the Holy Bible: *"Watch out for false prophets. They come to you in sheep's clothing, but inwardly they are ferocious wolves"* (Matthew 7:15).

Review this chapter in the book to aid you in helping your children learn to distinguish between positive and negative role models. Point out representatives of both groups. Use the following chart to assist you in teaching your children the differences between positive and negative behavior and to determine which role model they represent.

POSITIVE ROLE MODEL vs. WOLF IN SHEEP'S CLOTHING

POSITIVE ROLE MODEL BEHAVIORS	WOLF IN SHEEP'S CLOTHING BEHAVIORS
Believes in forgive and forget. Does not hold a grudge against others.	Always insists on taking control. Also very vindictive and seeks revenge at all costs.
Willing to listen to other points of view. Will ask questions to make sure they understand different perspectives.	Often very impatient. Not willing to wait for what they want. Will push/dare you to do or behave a certain way because it suits *their* needs/desires.
Recognizes that no one knows everything, that no one has all the answers. Accepts authentic criticism.	Does not like to be corrected by others. This makes them feel threatened. Fear losing control.
Has a sense of values that keeps them from going after what they want and hurting others to get it.	Willing to do or say whatever it takes to get what they want. Will twist the truth to suit their purposes.
Is willing to go out of their way to help others. Shows compassion and concern for others.	Knows what to say or do to gain trust very quickly. Uses this knowledge to manipulate others. If this doesn't work, they use guilt, shame, and fear to maintain control and get what they want.
Willing to admit mistakes and accepts responsibility for them. Works to correct them.	Will not accept responsibility for their bad behavior. *Will blame you for making them behave that way.*
Is loyal to those close to them, even in their absence.	Demands loyalty from others but refuses to reciprocate.
Recognizes that being kind and supportive with no expectations is a blessing to others and themselves.	**Does nothing without expecting something in return.**

1. Additional sources of help with this topic are: ***https://bit.ly/3DmetxFHeros and https://bit.ly/3FiTYm5Mentors.***

2. ***Discussions about "Little Red Riding Hood" fairy tale and its relevance to "wolf in sheep's clothing" and what real heroes do: https://bit.ly/3kFRy9kRed-Riding-Hood and https://bit.ly/3m8Pd7Nheros.***

CHAPTER FOUR REFLECTION AND NOTES

ENTER YOUR THOUGHTS/IDEAS/CONCERNS/REVELATIONS HERE:

_____

_____

_____

_____

_____

_____

_____

_____

CHAPTER FIVE

Practice What You Preach

*"You can know a lot of scripture and have the gift to teach,
but what is more important is to practice what you preach."*
—https://sermons4kids.com/practice_preach.htm

A re you *WALKING YOUR TALK?*

This chapter focuses on the importance of understanding how our words and actions come across to our children. Ask yourself the following questions (answer each question with a *Y* for yes or an *N* for no):

1. Have I ever said "do as I say, not as I do" to my children? (How did they react?) _____

2. Do I take advantage of *teachable moments* with my children? Reread this chapter for examples. _____

3. Do I apologize to others (including my children) when I learn I was wrong about something I thought they may have done or said? How do they react? _____

4. When I interact with my children, do I look ahead with the "Begin with the End in Mind" approach (Stephen Covey, The Seven Habits of Highly Effective People)? What do you want your children's future to be? _____

As you answer the questions above, refer to the charts in chapters one (Changing My Mindset Self-Assessment) and two (My Family-Culture Assessment). The answers to these questions may cause you to go back and reevaluate how you responded to questions/statements in those charts.

CHAPTER FIVE REFLECTION AND NOTES

ENTER YOUR THOUGHTS/IDEAS/CONCERNS/REVELATIONS HERE:

_____

_____

_____

_____

_____

_____

_____

_____

CHAPTER SIX

Don't Let Others Define You

*"Don't let others define you. **You Define Yourself.**"*
—Ginni Rometty

A positive mindset and a healthy outlook are key components in a strong sense of *self-esteem and self-worth*. However, it is nearly impossible to help our children develop a strong sense of self from an early age if *we, ourselves,* need help in these areas.

Your honest answers to the following questions give valuable insights into your self-esteem and self-worth (answer each question with a *Y* for yes or an *N* for no):

1. Do *you* tend to let others persuade *you* to do and say things you don't want to, but *you're* afraid they won't like/love *you* anymore if *you* don't? _____

2. Do *you* remain silent when someone takes advantage of *you*, not calling them on it because *you* don't want to upset them? Are *you* afraid of how they will react? _____

3. Do *you* always find *yourself* getting involved with people who are inconsiderate and insensitive to *you* and others? _____

4. Do *you* tend to find excuses for others' negative behavior towards *you*, even when *you* know it's not right? _____

5. Do *you* tend to allow others to tell *you* what *you* should think and do, even if *you* don't feel that way? _____

6. Do *you* know this is wrong, but *you* don't know how to turn things around? _____

Go back and read, or reread, this chapter in the book. *Consider the following as you do so:*

1. Have your children been suspended for behavior problems in school (fighting, bullying other students, not completing assignments, defying authority, etc.)? Why?

2. Do your children spend a lot of time alone, rather than interacting with other children? This could be a sign that they are being bullied in school but are afraid to report it.

3. Do you spend more time *criticizing* than **affirming** and supporting your children?

4. Review the **My Family-Culture Assessment** *chart* you completed in chapter two. Is there a connection between your responses in the chart and how you answered this chapter's questions?

5. Do you know who your children's friends are? Do you know anything about their friends' families?

6. Have you taught your children how to make wise choices in the friends with whom they associate? What about your friends? Would you want your children to emulate them? If the answer is no, why do *you* associate with those people?

What does it reveal about your self-esteem and self-worth as you read this chapter? Do you see a connection to your children's behavior?

1. For help, check out these resources: ***https://bit.ly/3FjlT5vSelf-Esteem and https://bit.ly/3kHATCaSelf-Esteem-Self-Worth.***

2. *A resource that highlights this topic: https://bit.ly/30uFb9fdonotdefineme.*

CHAPTER SIX REFLECTION AND NOTES

ENTER YOUR THOUGHTS/IDEAS/CONCERNS/REVELATIONS HERE:

_____

_____

_____

_____

_____

_____

_____

_____

CHAPTER SEVEN

I Don't Care About How Much You Know until I Know How Much You Care

—https://bit.ly/3rUQvabkidsdontcare

This chapter highlights the importance of ensuring our children feel love, especially from those closest to them. The following images bring this point home:

https://bit.ly/3rUQvabkidsdontcare

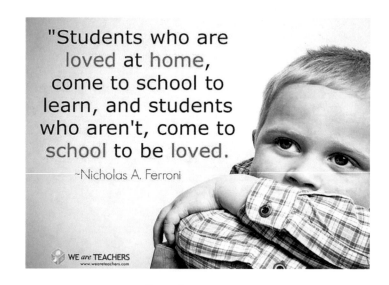

https://bit.ly/3rJFkAOstudentslove

Saying the words, *"I Love You,"* but not demonstrating with our actions makes the words seem hollow and meaningless to our children. Please review the list below. How often do you give your children what they want and need from this list? If you don't now, commit to doing as many as possible as part of your mindset transformation.

NINE THINGS KIDS WANT FROM PARENTS

1. *SHOWING IS BETTER THAN TELLING*—I learn by observing what you do/say every day.

2. *LOVE ME*— Give me hugs and kisses. You teach me to love others.

3. *KIND AND FIRM DISCIPLINE*—My brain is still developing, and so I'm slow in learning. But I do want to learn, if you patiently and kindly teach me.

4. *BE MY SAFE HAVEN*—Always be here for me, no matter what.

5. *TALK WITH ME*—Don't just talk to me.

6. *TRUST ME*—Let me make my own decisions on non-safety or health-related things. I couldn't learn to walk without falling. I can't learn to make good decisions without making bad ones.

7. *ENCOURAGE ME*—Your praise means so much to me.

8. *HEAR ME*—Sometimes I just want to be heard without judgment or lecturing.

9. *ACCEPT WHO I AM*—Don't constantly compare me to other kids.

NOTE: The statements above derive from "11 Things Kids Want From Parents" by Pamela Li, MS, MBA, ***https://www.parentingforbrain.com/raising-children/.*** I chose the words I felt were more relevant to the message I wanted to convey here. **Check out this resource for more on this subject:** ***https://bit.ly/30p395wHow-Much-You-Care.***

CHAPTER SEVEN REFLECTION AND NOTES

ENTER YOUR THOUGHTS/IDEAS/CONCERNS/REVELATIONS HERE:

_____

_____

_____

_____

_____

_____

_____

_____

CHAPTER EIGHT

Don't Ignore the Message Because You Don't Like the Messenger

It's not easy to accept advice from someone we may have had issues with in the past. This chapter discusses how important it is to evaluate *WHAT* is said, apart from the **WHO is** speaking. What advice/messages would you listen to now if you could go back? Who was the source? Use the chart below to list them:

MY *"IF I COULD GO BACK"* CHART

What was the Message?	Who was the Source?	Why did you Ignore it?	What happened as a Result?

1. **These resources can help keep you from repeating this mistake in the future:** *https://bit.ly/30qEaPFMessage-Messenger and https://bit.ly/3cePDDZListening-Skills.*

CHAPTER EIGHT REFLECTION AND NOTES

ENTER YOUR THOUGHTS/IDEAS/CONCERNS/REVELATIONS HERE:

_____

_____

_____

_____

_____

_____

_____

_____

_____

CHAPTER NINE

This Too Shall Pass

We all must deal with challenges in our lives. No one is immune. Some of the challenges we can foresee and prepare ourselves. Others seem to come from out of the blue. We are blindsided, knocked off guard. It is hard for us to believe that *"this too shall pass."* Imagine how difficult it must be for our children who have no experience.

Go back to your *Family-Culture Assessment* chart in chapter two. If your family culture allows your children to voice their honest feelings without fear of punishment, you have a better chance of helping them through their challenges.

1. This resource will help with many of the emotional issues that confront our children: ***https://bit.ly/31U5OoiEmotions.***

2. Sometimes we need added inspiration to help us get through the pain and hurt we may be feeling. For that, check out the resources below:

   https://bit.ly/3HAFro3Inspiration1

   https://bit.ly/30x6P5winspiration2

   https://bit.ly/3wSdIKyInspiration3

CHAPTER NINE REFLECTION AND NOTES

ENTER YOUR THOUGHTS/IDEAS/CONCERNS/REVELATIONS HERE:

_____

_____

_____

_____

_____

_____

_____

_____

CHAPTER TEN

Patience Is Still A Virtue

"Patience doesn't mean passivity or resignation, but power. It's an emotionally freeing practice of waiting, watching, and knowing when to act."
—**Judith Orloff, MD,** *The Empath's Survival Guide: Life Strategies for Sensitive People*

The need for *instant gratification* is a driving force behind many of our actions and behaviors in today's world. Too often, this leads to tragic outcomes we *cannot* reverse. This chapter focuses on how a negative mindset feeds the "I want it now" attitude.

Do you have an "I want it now" attitude? On a scale of 1 (totally disagree) to 5 (totally agree), rate your level of agreement with the following statements:

1. I don't care about what might happen later. When I want something, I want it now.

2. I spend at least 6 to 8 hours a day on my social media accounts because I *love* the immediate responses when sending out messages/posts.

3. When I go shopping, I don't compare prices. If I like it, I buy it then.

4. I know I should wait until I know more about _____ before we move in together/get married, but I like/love them, and they said they care about/love me.

What were your responses? How many statements did you rate at 4 or 5? Would you handle any of them differently now? Which ones and why?

When we practice what I call the 3Ps, *Positive Mindset + Patience + Preparation,* we save ourselves a ton of regret later.

Check out the following resources as you work towards managing your desire for *instant gratification:*

https://bit.ly/31Yyxs5Instant-Gratification

https://bit.ly/3kAAvp6Delayed-Gratification

https://bit.ly/3ovpOW6Patience

CHAPTER TEN REFLECTION AND NOTES

ENTER YOUR THOUGHTS/IDEAS/CONCERNS/REVELATIONS HERE:

_____

_____

_____

_____

_____

_____

_____

_____

CHAPTER ELEVEN

Decisions for Today vs. Tomorrow

"Make decisions that will create the future you desire."
—**Mike Murdock,** *The Leadership Secrets of Jesus*

When it comes to making important decisions—those decisions that can leave a lasting impact on our lives and the lives of those closest to us—we must remember *ONE SIZE DOES NOT FIT ALL.*

When we approach decision making with a *positive mindset*, we recognize the importance of evaluating *how* that decision could affect ourselves and others, both now and in the future. The *"Begin with the End in Mind"* approach **(Stephen Covey, The Seven Habits of Highly Effective People)** is needed here.

What approach do you take when making important decisions?

Complete the following chart in this manner:

1. *Put a checkmark in the appropriate response column for each question.*

2. *Enter the total number of checkmarks at the bottom of each column.*

MY *DECISION-MAKING APPROACH* CHART

Do I Take the Time to Ask Myself these Questions *Before* Making Important Decisions?	Rarely	Sometimes	Most of the Time	Always	Depends on Whom it Affects
Would this choice put me and others in danger?					
Would this choice cause someone else emotional hurt or pain?					
Does this choice go against my teachings about right and wrong?					
Would this choice cause my family or friends to be hurt or disappointed in me?					
Will this choice cause me to lose the respect of those close to me?					
Will my self-respect and self-worth be negatively impacted?					
Am I doing this out of anger or unkindness toward someone?					
Is my impatience driving this choice?					
Will this choice go against my religious teachings about how to treat others?					
Is this choice based on a desire to impress someone?					
Is someone pressuring me to make this choice before I am ready?					
How will I feel about myself tomorrow, after I've made this choice?					
Total of the number of checkmarks in each column:					

1. How do you feel about your current approach to making key decisions based on the results in the chart?

2. Are the outcomes of your important choices reflected in how you answered the questions in the chart?

3. Do your responses to any of the questions suggest that you should reevaluate how you make key decisions?

4. Which mindset do you think drives the way you make decisions right now?

Helping our children make good decisions is equally important. It is especially true as they make choices regarding their career and life goals. They need to recognize that not everyone will cheer them on, particularly some *family* members and *so-called* friends. Have you taught them how to recognize the differences between their *Inspirers* and their *Detractors?*

Complete the chart on the next page and share it with them.

INSPIRERS VS. DETRACTORS CHART

Inspirer's action	Who is an example?	Why?	Detractor's opposite action	Who is an example?	Why?
Celebrates your successes			Minimizes your successes		
Supports your efforts			Criticizes your efforts		
Looks for ways to help you			Looks for ways to distract you		
Helps you overcome obstacles			Refuses to help you overcome obstacles		
Offers a listening ear when needed			Tells you why you should quit		

1. After sharing the chart, how did your children react? Were they surprised?

2. Now that they know how to interpret the thinking and attitudes/mindset behind the actions of others, help your children keep their distance from those who are *NOT* their supporters/inspirers.

3. It is still important for you to help your children keep these things in mind as they encounter others along their journey to achieve their life goals.

CHAPTER ELEVEN REFLECTION AND NOTES

ENTER YOUR THOUGHTS/IDEAS/CONCERNS/REVELATIONS HERE:

_____

_____

_____

_____

_____

_____

_____

_____

_____

CHAPTER TWELVE

Where Do I Go From Here?

N ow that you have completed the guide and generated a ton of information about yourself and your family, you may be asking, *"What do I do now? I know a lot more now than I did when I began this journey, but I still don't know how to turn my life around. I still don't have a clue about where to start."*

You are now at the point where you must create your *Mindset-Transformation Action Plan* that will take you through the steps you need to build the future you desire and deserve for yourself and your family.

Before embarking on the steps you must take to achieve the life you want for you and your children, take the time to speak to your *inner being*. Find a quiet place and silently repeat the following phrases to yourself. They will help you *mentally* prepare for the work ahead of you.

- With *GOD* as my guide, I can achieve *ANYTHING!!!*
- I have the ability and the will to change my current mindset.
- I know that *"when I change the way I look at things, the things I look at change"* (*Wayne Dyer,* http://www.drwaynedyer.com/blog/success-secrets/). They go from negative to positive.
- I deserve to live a life of positivity.
- My family deserves to be happy and thrive.
- I am determined to achieve my desired outcome for myself and my family, despite our obstacles.
- I know that a positive mindset leads to proactive, positive action.
- I AM READY!!!

As Stephen Covey says, "Begin with the end in mind." Work with your children to answer the following questions:

- What do you want others to see when they look at you and your family?
- How do *you* want to feel about the changes you and your family have made?
- Ask your children how they *want* to feel about the changes your family has made?

Step 1—Review your answers to the questions above. Use your responses to complete step two.

Step 2—Create a *Family Vision Statement* with your children by completing the following:

By the end of _____ (enter a month/year), other family members and friends will notice a significant improvement in how we interact with them and each other. They will see (complete the sentence with what you want others to see):

_____

_____

Step 3—Paste a copy of your Family Vision Statement to the front of your *Mindset-Transformation Action Plan* as a constant reminder of why you are taking these critical steps.

Your vision statement should drive what *actions/behaviors* you need to change to make it come true. When you put a deadline on your Action Plan, it forces you to *ACT!*

The following template will help you map out the steps you and your children need to take to make your new family vision a reality.

As you develop your Action Plan, keep the following key points in mind:

- Nothing is more important than becoming the *positive role model* your children deserve.
- Lasting change takes time, effort, patience, and persistence. The 3Ps I referred to in chapter ten will apply here—*P*ositive Mindset +*P*atience + *P*reparation.
- Your *Accountability Partner* will be an important resource during your transformation journey.
- Remember, you must continue to *practice, practice, practice* your changed, more positive-minded approach to how you interact with your family, friends, and community.

Step 4—Complete developing your Action Plan.

Step 5—Begin carrying out your Action Plan.

Step 6—When you get stuck, ask God to guide you. Go back to the mental-preparation phrases you spoke to yourself, the ones from above, and talk to your **Accountability Partner.**

Step 7—Take time to celebrate breakthroughs as you make progress.

Step 8—Take pride in your accomplishments!!

Step 9—At the end of your journey, you may be eligible to receive a special *Certificate of Completion* (see sample below).

NOTE: This certificate is presented to those who participate in a facilitated parenting session. If you are taking this journey on your own, you should still celebrate with family and friends, recognizing your tremendous achievement!!!

My Mindset-Transformation Action Plan

My Family Vision Statement					

Short-Term Goal (Achieve 30 Days from Action-Plan Start Date)

Step(s) I will take to Achieve My Goal	Time line (Start/End Dates)	Expected Outcome	Who Will Help Me?	Actual Outcome	Did I Achieve My Goal (Y/N)? Why?

Comments:

Mid-Term Goal (Achieve 60 Days from Action-Plan Start Date)

Step(s) I will Take to Achieve My Goal	Time line (Start/End Dates)	Expected Outcome	Who Will Help Me?	Actual Outcome	Did I Achieve My Goal (Y/N)? Why?

Comments:

Long-Term Goal (Achieve 90 Days from Action-Plan Start Date)

Step(s) I will Take to Achieve My Goal	Time line (Start/End Dates)	Expected Outcome	Who Will Help Me?	Actual Outcome	Did I Achieve My Goal (Y/N)? Why?

Comments:

Next Steps:

CERTIFICATE

OF COMPLETION

This Certificate is Proudly Presented to

Name of Participant

For successfully completing the Parenting Program

Awarded on the {Enter Date Here}

Doris Barren
COURSE FACILITATOR

{Name of Program Director}
NAME OF PROGRAM

PARTING THOUGHTS

Remember the following:

1. None of us is perfect, but with *GOD* as our guide and the support of family and friends, we can do *ANYTHING*!!

2. *YOU* are the first and most important *ROLE MODEL* in your children's lives.

3. Your parenting role doesn't end when your children become adults; it evolves.

4. If you find yourself falling back into old habits (we all regress at times), don't despair. Revisit your chapter charts and your Action Plan (remember, this is a living document).

5. Our children *LEARN WHAT THEY LIVE EVERY DAY!*

6. "If it doesn't *CHALLENGE* you, it doesn't *CHANGE* you" (Fred DeVito, https://bit.ly/3lChvHachallenge).

7. "I am not what happened to me. I am what I *choose* to become" (Carl Gustav Jung, https://bit.ly/3G9W6x4Choosetobe).

8. You are *NOT* alone!!

If you have participated in a *Parenting Session*, please complete the *Participant Feedback Survey* provided by the facilitator. If you completed this guide independently, don't hesitate to contact me directly. My email address is **dorisbarren@ymail.com**. I value and appreciate your input, which helps me improve!!!

PEACE AND BLESSINGS TO ALL WHO READ AND USE THIS GUIDE AS THEY WORK TO TRANSFORM THEIR MINDSET AND RESTORE THEMSELVES AND THEIR FAMILIES!!!

Doris Barren

LET US WALK THE PATH FROM DARKNESS INTO THE LIGHT TOGETHER!!

https://unsplash.com/images/feelings/inspirational

kenny-s-7qRM11Kmnh4-unsplash.jpg

We Thank God, from Whom All Our Blessings Flow, for Getting Us this Far!!!

REVIEWS

"This workbook will benefit many parents in guiding each to recognize and make any needed changes to increase their own 'positivity' to help influence children to grow into successful individuals who will, in turn, help their communities. Doris Barren is doing wonderful work to help conversations and healing start so we can all help future generations. This process starts with each of us as we understand the importance of helping all the children around our world."

Lisa Jones

CEO | Co-Founder at Global Goodwill Ambassadors Foundation (GGAF)

"Raising kids is difficult; there's no question about it. Without the right help, things can seem dire, but that's where "Change Your Mindset/Save Your Child: Saving Our Children By Healing Ourselves" comes in. Author Doris Barren has given us a comprehensive guide, the ultimate guide, to monitor our children's growth and well-being. This reading will be a staple of parenting literature, and one of those books that we simply cannot miss in our libraries."

- Ann Collins, Book Reviewer

CPSIA information can be obtained
at www.ICGtesting.com
Printed in the USA
BVRC101056150222
628969BV00003BB/22